Caravaggio's Kimono

Caravaggio's Kimono

KEN FIFER

Contents

for Elizabeth and Ben

Caravaggio's Kimono
The Rest on the Flight into Egypt

Friends, and by friends I mean anybody not
offended by kimonos in the desert or watching
angels play squatters to sleep. . . . In the harmonious
moment between felonies when the sky
withdraws replaced by music,
thank you for visiting Caravaggio and me
at *Be and Let Be* Spa & Wellness
in Macungie PA across the street
from Lehigh County's murmuring
recycling pond, waves that
bubble and pulse at dusk, all
base elements transformed. Who'd
have guessed you'd be stopping here to rest
and choose a new dress for your flight
into Egypt? Maybe a few. Nevertheless
allow me to welcome you. Past
the aisles of ready-to-wear, past
Herod's decrees bombers above battlefields Mickey
Mouse piano keys and everything you've
worn before, you'll arrive at last at
Caravaggio's kimono, a monster
hero beast drawn free
hand in red and yellow dyes folded
in the shape of a sleeping bear. Why not try
it on? Or like Frank Lloyd W, would
you prefer wisteria embroidered
on trellises? After all, it's your last
resort too. Welcome to the half
light at the edge of the miasma
where every moment invents its own
bliss.

In Guo Xi's *Early Spring*

Spring arrived unexpectedly with plenty
of blame to go around. In the outer
boroughs where brownouts run
amok, I spied a pack of zeros
winking in the dark. I guess
you'd call it winking. I scrawled
their names on 3 × 5 cards. I don't
grasp why, but being
caught in the ricochet of release
and collision reminded me of Guo Xi's
black-and-white landscapes, mainly
the one called *Early Spring*. Loneliness so
luxuriantly empty, empty
spaces became clouds. In a doorway a river
forked through my forehead. My green
lips split like swollen twigs.

Making Love at Marconi Station

There's no cypher subtle enough.
We're breathless on the Atlantic sea wall
where the beach goes out dash dash dot.
After the last whale sinks into place
dead stations appear on these waves.
Everything that vanishes stays.
Codes collapse. Breakers break.
Silence saves will save has saved
us, so far, so far away, when neither
words nor wireless may.

The @s of your %s

The :)s in my email remind me our
actual lives are also
composed of punctuation
and of punctuation's sonnets, none
more beautiful than "The @s
of your %s that looked
) (have turned ( )…." When
I hear you, my eyebrows
^. The &s
perch on feeders at first,
then bolt, forming <s. When
the dark #s widen above the
| and the river ~s over
each + leaving countless ?s your
presence rises more: than =. When the night
sky resembles a gray
scroll-lock key pressed
to tell us where and how insert
an ! for every *. Shift . to >. I promise
not to say a word.

The Jewel of Berks County

Ten
categories of competitive yodeling. When
I ask why, she purses her lips. If
it's said at all she wants it
yodeled. *Dot is dot.* She's
a daughter of the dotters of wisdom
and winner of the Under
Twenty Hill to Hill. But even
as far off as Macungie,
grandpas on benches, reading
children's books with hardened
eyes and almost no lips, upon hearing
her warble press their tongues
to gums for spit and brace
themselves for an eleventh
yodel — part
rescue, part lift, part
egress, part crypt, part
substance, and all
mist and itch. And even
if her voice doesn't carry
to Lyons from Blue Mountain
Motors, I still know she's there
leaning over the hood, yodeling
to the engine in her polkadot
Capris — the Jewel
of Berks County trying to get
the old Dodge tuned. Even
when I dream I'm Cezanne, her trill
comforts me. She knows two
large fries from Sheetz, one
for now and one as needed, will help
me forget l'Orangerie and picnic

baskets along the Seine. She says
La Santé hosts actual food
fights, with Apollinaire
and the Algerians, with Jean
Genet and Paul Verlaine.

Your Lucky Life
for Stern

In your sailor hat and pea coat you cross
the asphalt and see what you thought
was your home is a derelict boat.
From the prow what was
a black locust turns out to be a Jacob's
ladder. When you climb
down, you imagine you're in Washington
Crossing State Park, but actually you
are on your own porch in Raubsville thanking
Pat for the tuna on rye. Lean
back, sip
your Schlitz, look at the river, shift
your chair among the ornamental pillars that
hold up the gabled roof. As if
whatever comes your way leaves
your prints: when locusts slump
and noisy maples dig in
to grow bored and
windy along the pointless
Delaware, when banister paint
peels from your palms, when black
and white sparrows leave no
tracks at all, you believe they're all
your countrymen. When moles
tunneling under your sills smack
their lips, with the river this close they
must be your blood. When you bite
into your sandwich you savor
the pleasure and ache of harvested grain
in silos where the light goes down. You
can taste the gaff
in your cheek, the fishy

vicissitudes, the last
moments of tuna roused from
the deep, that fit so fault
lessly into your mouth.

Cryology

In 1611 Kepler invented snowflakes: *to*
imagine an individual soul for each
and any starlet is utterly absurd. Crystals,
columns, needles, and plates, every
snowflake looks the same
on a frozen hill above
a frozen lake. When I found
your name on an envelope
a moment of clarity and whiteness
reached inside me like a toothache, one
of many those weeks without you, when it
was impossible to know if my elbow
suffered from an actual bruise or just
from reaching out
over and over. The wind
blowing through my coat made
it difficult to remember. I ran
with the water under the ice, heard
more than saw the dark's surprising still
green moss and fallen white
pine needle stars. If I had six
legs I'd be three dancers. If I had six
fingers I'd know why snowflakes
danced like Graces, still
attired in Grecian robes.

On the Fault Line

1950s Spanish Harlem

In the Projects I needed antidotes, anecdotes, Sherpa's
stones to slip through the chain
link fence and horn talismans to string
around my waist to put me on the right
elevator. I needed a friend
in the mar-proof halls because if
I hesitated I'd be lost and have no
choice but to point at flag
decals on apartment doors. Each
bell *rings* in an old country. Each
bell rings *in* an old country.
I believed the Projects were my chance
to become a ski bum masked and willing
to risk the next
avalanche, dropping fingers, losing
toes, to sniff
at the winds off the crust where the moon
marked snowdrifts bank. I wanted to
wander among yaks
and yetis on a snowblind
pass without a plan to arrive intact. *98th
and Lex.* I yelled *Watch
your step* as I scrambled
to the lip of the next crevasse.

Departure

Because it's called *Departure*
the mothers at the MOMA
have put it in the third floor corner
corridor. What
do you say to Max Beckmann when they hang
Falling Man upside down? Dear
Max, we have hung your most
beautiful *Departure*
by the elevators where
families stop to ask the guard *Where's*
Guernica? Where? They don't care
about your overpainted hero
with the lamp, the mutilated
child, the Holy
Ghost with visor drawn. I could sit
in the Sculpture Garden and watch
the city weekdays for hours.
I could lose myself in *Water Lilies* and stare
through the windows in front of Monet.
But to admire the only Max Beckmann I must
learn to loiter
among the litter of departure
between pissoirs
and glass elevator doors.

Like the Stone Moses Paralyzed

on the Pope Julius Tomb we can't
get across the silence without
interlude. Our alphabets run
off the page into the space after words. I mean
our dusks and daybreaks run
off. To an empty wire coat hanger
as soon as you step out you're lost. In
the thermos on your left I'm cold
and hoarse in my outdoor thirst. In
the ashtray taken away and returned
we are a flash of heat and the flesh
of ash. I polished
silverware after you left, watched
daylight leak through Depression
glass. Looking out over the sink
I drifted away. Forgetting
the special fire we're made of
we're ashamed and later bored. After forty
years of stones and thirst, after anger
like a wilderness, why don't we
pull in our horns?

Gloss

Concerning Bihzad's miniature
birds and cats—as
soon as readers see his name they
turn the page that I can't. And for those
who remain, before
they get through my gloss of *Our
cats want to be change
agents* and *Unintended birdseed
effects*, a few
more TVs will light up,
though probably not
enough to cause local
brownouts. And even
if they do and their
screens flicker and they
wind up powerless and bored, how
many will reach
The sparrows gliding above us dream
and get off on
the whole cat/bird thing before they fall
into abrupt nods? A few
maybe, but after that comes *Picking
through the minor debris*,
when even the most
resolute will lose heart and drift
away before waking hours later
slumped over *Peterson's
Field Guide to Birdseed*. As far
as we can see there's nothing
here except you and me
listening to each other breathe.

According to the Baal Shem Toad

even frogs are croaking for me,
squeaking away, improbable chorus,
floating like brown leaves, noses
exposed. *The point is*
singing and not hearing. The point is
hearing and not grasping — one
frog's thoughts leap the thoughts
of the next, drawing out their commentaries.
They stare as frogs stare, past bare trees
into the brown and broken leaves. In a few
weeks the same leaves frogs believe will be
turning green and starting over. Frogs think
of frogs as leaves of course, but more
often think of leaves as frogs, with
a different speech of another order, probably
cousins once removed. *Philo*
sophically, one frog
sings, *philosophically they must*
be frogs because of their beauty,
by right of their intelligence and music,
by virtue of their webbed feet, lithe
bodies, splashy techniques, more
dry and severe, less quick and sweet,
but all in all pure amphibian. Each
prolongs the breath in one key, each
arranges the air in short leaps, each
so to speak exhales a new
leaf. The point is,
if I sing, nothing
that croaks can be foreign to me.

The Soote Season

As in Surrey's poem, the sweet
season muddies the hill
and swamps the ditch, but did his night
ingales *with feathers new* peck at his
window like my turkeys do? Or try to
hide behind a blade
of grass? Turkeys
aren't *turtles*. They're not *soote*.
Tremors that ripple through their wings begin
with an itch and end with a rash.
Guided by a hoarse inner voice, the songs
they launch are short but good. They sound
a lot like wood on wood. Turkeys flap,
hop twice, and flop
before they regain their stuff and strut
nonchalant asses into the brush.

Rosalind

thinking Orlando, whose
father's spirit keeps roiling, too
much, *furioso*, his whole
act more jakes than Jacques, she already
knows what daddies want — wrestling,
vengeance, props, and pomp, mass
transfers of bewildered bodies, bodies
to be chunked and stacked. Why
wave off less delicate hominids if he
insists on ignoring the obvious? She
needs a little less drama. She says,
Fathers always linger. Now and then
they give us the finger. Let's
vamoose and learn to forage.

Ash

Supercharged by distress
ash put their energy entirely into sex. Seedlings
are coming up everywhere. She
says, *Seedlings are coming*
up everywhere, and she wants
me beside her, bent
close to the earth, as we pop
clumps up and let them drop. We can't
stop what happens next — an all
ash issue of *Fine Gardening*, an installation
at the Whitney, a super PAC called *Save*
Our Ash, Congressional
hearings, defense
contracts.

A Saturday Mow

When the power mowers slow
we can hear the year turn, reminding
us to look up at the clouds. Shouldn't we
turn the sprinklers on? This
Saturday is *comme un rêve*. Every
man jack sports red and black
in a passion play for root
and branch. Let each
prepare a little mound. Yellow
trucks with wind machines already
here collecting leaves roll
triumphant block on block.

Walnuts

I've seen squirrels throw them down.
Before the chattering's done they're gone.
I must piece together seed and shell
or the walnut tree grows unrecognizable.
Look at me, leaves in one hand, thin
air in the other, mouth stuffed with pins,
bits of duct tape stuck to sleeves,
going out on a limb, trying not to
be mistaken for a thief or a Tom
peeping through a window left ajar.

Three for Ahmet Ada
after Ada

Maybe the Man

Arbor: Where apple trees go to think?
Ardor: Why trees wear pink?
Ahmet Ada: Why pace from room to room?
Alphabet: Alzheimer's aubade afternoon?
Maybe the man called Ahmet Ada doesn't
exist: Always
the other, the easternmost. Maybe, who
knows, his sorrows will lift.

This Frivolous Voice

of the fig and the pomegranate close
to the sea at the far
end of the city mixes
with barking in the long
tranquility of his garden. Last
year, sad trees told Ahmet
Ada their dreams. This
year, robust and serene, they're not
saying anything. Evening's
withdrawing into the headland.
Evening's holding on
to its knees. *Mmm,*
Ahmet says, *Mmm.* You
need to speak
Turkish to
get the hang of what
it all means.

Past the Shore

Amazed by it all, the plow
headed for the sea, the sky's
fishing line, a single
sunray dangling down through summer
shade, a boy in a hat stares
at the sea too long. Seagulls
bob and weave. A fisherman
mends his nets and forgets.
The boy fidgets a little
less. They're all preparing
for the voyage. The sky's
a cotton reverie. I shake
off my flip-flops and step
past the shore where air
and water form one seam. A seed
pod blows out over the waves. What
are these boats and birds and seeds? Why
are we dressed in mortal cloth?

Salvation Has a Use-by Date

Caravaggio's Nativity with St. Francis and St. Lawrence *(stolen from the Oratory of San Lorenzo in Palermo, October 16, 1969)*

In his final nativity, Michaelangelo
Merisi da Caravaggio, always
the lost one, never
looking where
he ought, fixes his concupiscent
eyes on a redneck Joseph and spins
the brim of the cuckold's country
hat into the painting's lone
halo. The baby looks
past his mother's face at an angel dangling
down from brown heaven, its
body wrapped in a few
Latin words. Or maybe
the ox interests him more. In a barn
full of saints, Caravaggio,
a paint-slinger drawn by a farmer,
an accessory to crimes of the future, shows
off his tights and recalibrates.

Carracci's Violin

In his red chalk study
for *The Baptism of Christ,*
the violin's already there
waiting for an angel's grip.
But boy and bow and violin
are missing in the finished
altarpiece. Instead there's
the ordinary rock
and water, a baby's ass, a bent
tree on a distant cliff, and
in the corner, where the angelic
boy might have been, a scruffy
codger looks away, as if
lost in Carracci's
violins.

Scarabs by Lamplight

When we put caps on beetles
to keep them from looking up at stars
they get confused and wander. A featherweight
of remorse fills their hearts. So
scarabs on a cloudy Egyptian night
scan the *Times* for amulets and post
selfies to *The Book of the Dead #dungbeetles*. One
third of the species on Earth are beetles. Stars
in the Milky Way speak to them. *Beware*
the heart like a restless leg. On
the boat of Ra pixilate
your face. Astral
and horny, they wait
for the sky to clear. Immortality looks
like shit to them.

Shiners

Waters Meet, Ricketts Glen State Park, PA

At Waters Meet it's no breeze,
rising from stones after falling asleep.
Silence grows unthinkably thin
while shiners flash and fan their fins
for the least of things in the water's dish—
lines and circles, indecipherable signs.
I have a thought but waters cloud it.
I have a thought but can't pronounce it.
Waters Meet collides steep creeks
pooling dark around downed pine
in shallows water striders glide
when all their legs can't bring them ease.

Please Keep Hands Of* the Doors

Darker hearts do off with roses
but not with a bag of red nuts—
the lost F stops
in the tunnels of New York. F
knew the windows were
not doors even
though the darkness knocked. *She*
loves me loves me not. Pistachio
shells are what F counts, petals
cracked to red F's mouth. The lost
bass clef. The sixth
emptiness. F whose
door has fallen off.

Locomotive

There's an Amtrak engineer doing straight time
inside your striped hat and gunmetal eyes.
Like a beard you cannot outgrow and a
fire you can't put out, the angry
whistles of your breath—
your skin, my
friend, so
fair, so
dark.

À l'Orangerie

Juice doesn't dribble down my chin
when I eat fruit with Renoir, it drips
discretely from the side of my mouth. The only
darkness allowed at table are shadows
wrapped in linen.
When I press their cloth
to the arc
of my mouth, I taste the moment
boulevards begin. Fruit
goes all over my lap when I lunch
with Cezanne. When I reach
for an orange, he starts to shake.
I'm a poor man who overspent
on wallpaper and can't make ends meet. You can't,
he tells me, *forget the smell of milk*
fed human kindness after
it's been spilled. There's only one
knife and one napkin.

As I Am I See

But I don't see you ardent
librarian. Not
in the redacted lists marked
Unreturned. Neither
in the stacks nor
catalogued among *Overdue*
entries. So I go
down to the coast and flop
on my back to catch the laughter
of the rocks and watch
for blue words among rowboats
made of clouds. When the Sea
of Tranquility backlights
a pelican, I'll rise. I'd like to
be part of a larger loneliness.

Somewhere Else You're Getting Dressed

Armholes without
arms, sleeves without
wrists, folding
clothes, it's your body
I miss. I conjure
you dressed in your
pure repose which
you sewed inside
out to improve
the fit. Betsy, your
absence unsettles
the laundry whose
seams once circled
your breasts and
ribs. Buttonholes
wink at your more
tender buttons. I
stare at your
pocket and
pick at the lint.

In the Little Plazas

where our bodies part
we leave a series of memorial
arches that we march
under, avoiding cheap
shots, without any
scheme to recant
or recount. We raise
and lower flags and move
our bodies to the same
measure, the same flute
and tuba arrangement that
first occurred to John
Sousa — sweaty thoughts, knees
that knock, paths that
cross left to right, arms
and legs that intersect
at a city center, our
bodies paraded,
braided, all brass.

Man of Many Penises

That's him, the man
of platitudes, man of pluralities, man
in a caucus. Slippery
as a young pig in spring, anything
I say he says more
than once. He watches me.
Is there a *bissel*
in the abyss? I reflect on
his kisser in
a beveled blotchy
bathroom mirror. When one
penis is not enough,
asking for more is asking
too much, too much
piss, too few kidneys,
too few heads to ease out of
bed and stare through all
the windows at once.

How I Came to Pennsylvania

Two years later I moved to Pennsylvania.
It wasn't only for the fracking. It was
a risk I had to take. Grown
tired of my suburban tree, my true
desire was to extinguish the Centralia
fires, prevent the next
Three Mile, prepare
for another cycle
of Legionnaire's and Prayer
Riots, and dry
the damps of the Avondale
Mine. Caught
on the Jersey border between
haste and frantic haste, I was pulled
over by a Trooper on 378, wrong
time, wrong place. We were
almost face to face. *Remain
in the vehicle.* He slow
walked to his cruiser
wiping his shades.

The Invention of the Parachute

Allentown, PA

Over Red Cross buns and too
hot coffee I catch
your face in the *Morning Call* and fold
the page across your brow. Brave
parachutist, I'd have to be Gerald
Stern, an EMT, or a Da Vinci
Mentor at the Science Center, to picture
you, out of the blue, float into this circulation
radius, deciphering updrafts, breaking
news for those who pack their own
chutes. Here's the skinny: Iron
Pigs win 8–2, a chance of rain, un
explained stabbings on Fourth
and Chew, and overhead on page eight
you have just
jumped newborn out of the plane.

A Fountain for the Perplexed

Welcome to Bethlehem, the new
dispensation, built around
a steel mill in eastern
PA, a place to pass through on your
way Midwest, when
even your tires whine *Akron, Akron.*
You're hoping
for The Giant Tire, symbol of
Firestone and the wheel of time,
but instead find The Pilgrim's Fountain. *Let
the Traveler Be Refreshed.* Dry
spigot and dusty basin form
the subtext: execution
modifies intent. Before
buckling, consider alternatives. Motor
off to further restlessness to photograph
double distelfinks on 22 West, or hang
around to drink from this
fountain instead.

Watermarks

Water presents itself as a darkening
cloud, an immodest partner over
flowing the passage, a tear
in the eye of a dampening
wind. I find
the words *The arrival
of water!* leaning to one
side, already underway. *Wish
I may, wish I might*, in May
our body fluids shout. Cue
Maimonides and *The Chinese
Brothers*. To begin, eaves
drop on water. Remember the orphan
hitting the rock. Dive in head
first to salvage a message
from a mouthful of spit: submersion
is subversion and water's
a list, a way,
a fire, a taste,
a tap of weightlessness.

Love in a Time of Drought

By the dry creek bed in front of our door I can't
hear a stinkbug buzz or even
find a cloud in the sky. Under
willows, along headwaters, in
the depressions left by vernal ponds, among
sensitive ferns and jack-in-the-pulpits and umbrella
plants hung out to dry, stupefied
by heat, at the edges of fleabane and briar, I find neither
newt nor frog . . . until
out of the blue, thirteen wild
turkeys, too big and loud, march single
file onto the lawn, stare
at you sideways, and plop
down rustling in the shade to wait. Even wild
turkeys, the dumbest of birds, see
through you, daydreaming rain,
streams, lakes, well water hosed into tin
pie plates. They already
taste the grapes in their mouths.

Last Spring We

planted cactus, never
thinking it'd cause a drought. This
spring it was Siberian iris,
now the whole valley's snow
bound. We don't hash
over collective farming but want
to have old promises kept. We spout
passages from *The Cherry Orchard* until
we believe we're back
on the steppes. The difference
between a garden and a gulag? Salt
trucks in the iris beds.

All Night Murkiness

seeps through late March swamps,
nights that turn in
glutinous masses, black as black
moth wings tipped white.
That night I forget which
corpse exhaled me, which heart
shaped mouth spit me out.
Nights spent in true
moth devotions chew holes
in the sleeves of swamp roses, repeat
secrets that reveal seasons that respond to each
change of light. Last night, nameless
ferns rooted in run-offs and small
rain, expecting soon
to disappear, as so much
does these days all night.

Discontent in West Lafayette

In the rural morning racket the silent
city haunts me, worn out by the un
differentiated scenery, tired of following
my salary into the remote, the eastern
sky slung over my shoulder, the mud
cliffs rising fragrant and damp, the sand
and grit casting yellow
paths. Where's the steel
wilderness and blue exhaust, the grey
storied offices and high
shadowed walls? Days
decompose, missing letters, ellipses,
eclipses, obscure country nights.

Key

Perhaps like me you like to dream
of nights filled with raised
animal shapes, skeletons
in constellations, wolves,
monkeys, whales, snakes, time
breaking into fine particles. Perhaps,
like you, I like to dream I'm at
an offshore soda factory
collecting data that measure
sparkle. Spinning in the transparent
deep, the key is being extra
quiet. Not
marooned. Transformed.

She Wants to Be Spanish

So I ask who, who
else but you, could
be vacationing in Macungie among the thrifty
Amish, stealing hearts at the *Be*
and Let Be on New Sewage
Treatment Road? Like
the moon, we're recycled, not lost. We're not
a mirage inside a miasma, we're
in Marbella, where every
one's skinny. I'm not
lisping, I'm Andalusian, cycling
by in my black
lace cap.

Reservations

For people like me, the cartographers' lists
tremble and shift as each place-name insists
on its own narrative. From The Dingle
to Grand Forks, Great Falls to Great Karroo,
I stand at Lost & Unclaimed counters to page
and be paged, intent on my chits. Travel
alert, aircraft inert, from
Everest to Picayune, Kish to Qom,
Little Rock to Boulder and Eureka,
from Bergen op Zoom to Katmandu,
I depart for a place chosen
by how it sounds on my lips.

Triplet

A whitewashed room hides the
scent of resin dropped by mastic
trees on the streets of Ayvalik.

What Sugar Maples Tap and Turn In

Parke County, Indiana

Root shine sinks into the earth's
tips and edges up, greens,
first clues from underground. Wet
for dry the perishable
trades renovate the soil, survive as canned
goods down chain store aisles. Care
for the man entire. While stone
stars glide beneath Parke
County and white grubs fly the heavier
air of March's other skies, we
gather above them, start
wood fires, boil the dark
out of subterranean winds.

Against Gardens

The dark art of weeding,
reaching under
the earth to grab the root, doesn't
mean that much to me now. It's part
laziness, part arthritis, part
rapport with weeds, but more it's the play
of light on their leaves and the speed with
which they exhale tiny flowers. I twig
their need to go on, the way of jewel
weed and goldenrod, their need to
persist, despite limited gifts, that compel
them to seed hostile ground. When
they raise their voices
in a new chorus and organize
the yard with their booming bull
horns and homemade signs, I'll
be with them—without you, hypocrite
reader, you green-thumbed scab—
I'll be out there walking the line.

Poison Ivy

Rhus radicans

Beacon among shady perennials
and most persistent *Rhus* of all, I hope
you're happy now I'm
moist and weepy as you. Like
a butterfly to milkweed
and an old man to manure, I'm led
on by your red springs, your green
summers, your coy wide
eyed white
berried falls. Masks, long
pants, high gloves, rubber
bands on my wrists
and ankles, your smile
irresistible, I'm just
a pink thought in green shade.

Black-Eyed Susans

Rudbeckia hirta

stare me down in September. Fall
seems less
seed than stem. Leafless,
bent, stalk and cone, I don't get
their words, slurred or dubbed
or overheard. And I won't,
or mostly don't, flushed
by their rude beckoning.

For You

Past tiny grottos of dropped consonants,
in caves closed by avalanches, by the snaking
hollows of underground
rivers, by the snaking
hollows of underground texts, what
you heard last night wasn't a storm, wasn't
an ocean of churning blue moiré, wasn't
the future pulling out its own teeth—that
was me hoping to woo you by reciting Tristan
Tzara. *Here
is sand here is my body*—the one that
burned then deliquesced. My sadness
leaks from pebbles on this
uninhabited peninsula where I
try to hear what can't be said.

Indifference

Last leaves, grey rain, pale distances —
not long before, we've been over this.
Between regrets, between false starts,
come with us, come dear hearts,
and do not ask us who we are,
knowing already the transit of our star is
predictable and mysterious.
The sky is narrow, steep, star-rigged.
Pure indifference forces us.
We wear our lives like amulets.

The Consolation of Biology

According to the *New York Times*,
in Antarctica the algae thrive
despite twenty feet of water
beneath twenty feet of ice
from the bottom of their valley lakes
beneath several thousand feet of sky
in the submerged ferocity
of their passive pure biographies
they step up to the surface and embrace
in great cold and tiny light.

Trilobites

Lehighton, PA

My son and I leave early
with chisels and brushes
to collect fossil trilobites
with diminutive crowns,
secret keepers of the deep
who shouldered the sediment
long ago, now exposed inside Blue
Mountain, where a million
trilobites rose above
Lehighton to stare
at the moon breaking
through Silurian clouds. We don't
churn in slime or roll compound
eyes, but we turn to the same
star. Returning home on the Northeast
Extension and old 209, winding
through wind-and-water gaps, Ben
ascends into a sleep overflowing
with trilobites and moon
crabs, beams
flashing highway signs.

In Ankara I Smell the Story of Lost Love

What to say about these gatherings
in the basements of a thousand chicken
restaurants where groups of shy
Turks, you among them, defend
the return of cumin and whisper
the ascent of thyme. *Tell them we're not*
Saudi Arabia. Tell them we're not
barbarians. Last night, I scoped a dog
shot in the market and dragged
out of an ornate fountain where
it had splashed and growled after showing
off its jaws all week. In a strange
burg there's always a risk. What
can you do when all the squares and traffic
circles are deliciously
draped with dried intestines? I'm so
busy following my nose with my feet I forget
all about my American teeth.

Hats

A snapshot of my friend Nesrin sipping bitter
coffee outside a café in the bright Turkish light.
In her feathered millinery she
looks both flighty and burdened. When the great
Ataturk ruled, he remade the state. Nesrin's
grandmother woke one day illiterate
in a second alphabet, her grandfather's shorn
face reborn in another continent. In Turkey
beards are back; it's America's
turn to legislate
hats — turbans converted
into Stetsons, fezzes resewn
as baseball caps.

Flor de Noche Buena

for Joel R. Poinsett, horticulturalist and first US ambassador to Mexico

I desire the flower that means
good night. Free
lighting from the turpentine
tree, frankincense doesn't
interest me, and unpronounceable stiff
necked myrrh is better off
left buried. But your flower,
Mr. Ambassador, your shrub
of moist ravines, is the true
pride of our nation despite
its dopey leaves. The entire
diplomatic core should take
a tip from you — it's grace
and light renew
our soils, defoliants won't
do. So
gracias Joel R. Poinsett, though some
say you're a Red, you refused
to sow and reap bad dreams and cross
bred bracts instead. If half, just
half, our diplomats had
taken up your trowel and spread
their bullshit on the ground, the whole
earth would flower.

Fooling the Angel

When grandma fell sick, her
parents changed her name
in order to fool the Angel
of Death. They peeled her
an orange, not to
cure her but to let her taste
light and warmth before the Angel
returned. And as she chewed,
they said, *How worthless
girlchildren are*, trying to
avoid the Evil Eye. They shipped
her to New York, not
far from Yankee Stadium,
a place an Angel might
not look right away. In her first
American photos, just weeks
off the boat, she paid
to pose before a buffalo herd
and teepees painted on a screen. Fringed
buckskin, beadwork
boots, a cowgirl
hat, and leather chaps
seemed neither wasteful
nor strange, but a necessary
expense, her most
likely defense, better
than the rented white
handled pistols. Returning today
to Houston Street, a buckaroo, no
longer a greenhorn, I'm just another
Yankee with two names, one
for real and one to say, hoping to
find Miss Liberty too,

while the Angel looks
the other way.

At the Terminal

As enormous windows turn
to mirrors at dusk, I wait,
I've waited, I will wait. I'm doing
the dance of an airport man pacing
on the far side of the gate. I'm not
up for the open blue. The sky's
got beaks and beady
eyes. Plummet. Free
fall. That's my take.

Finding Bones in the Garden

Not exactly the migration I was hoping for. I dreamt
about birds made of broken glass, almost
blue, almost moonlight, the moon a suddenly
faraway bird come down to the hills in a lunar
slick of backlit swallows — bird
bones in flight in the hospital
garden between the ICU
and the canteen — a smudge
of crows still
stuck to their shadow in a sludge of fading
goo, flocking to be
discharged soon. Who'll
stop to take me home? I've pushed
away my only friend, no one
left to ask but skeletons.

Eurydice Chorus

Like a black dog at the shore's
sharp edge, I prick
my ears, watch my step, listen
to the water barking, move my right
foot near my left. *Bodies*
that return to grass. Bodies
of fire. Bodies of ash. Like a drowning
rat before its tiny grotto, clawing
awkwardly at dirty water, I twitch
like a finless fish, circle,
gnaw, breathless, spent. *Weak,*
strong, charmed, or strange, charged
or uncharged, bodies change. My
sweetheart haunts the forest
edge, exposing herself and squeezing
her breasts. There's no angelic guest, no
contagion worth the sores. *Bodies of muck.*
Bodies of water. Bodies
of love. Governing bodies. Bodies
for Eurydice sinking
in a fen among small ferns. No one
strays, I hear her singing, nothing
stays that touches earth. *Galactic*
bodies. Tibetan saints. Bodies waiting
in front of each gate. Spiders
climb our body fibers. Red ants carry
off small breaths. Life is short. We fuck
like crazy. Who
could ask for anything less?

My Mind Fallen from a Flowering Tree

In his unfinished miniature *Assault on a Castle*, Bihzad
places me among plumed soldiers showered
down upon by molten pitch while the enemy
advances past the last
drawbridge. I can't
bear to watch the prince in his tower perfectly
postured, unruffled against
a backdrop of puckering clouds. Bihzad stirs
pennants on the parapets that knot
the edges of the earth / air kilim blood
red, black, and summer green. For
painters and princes it's all in the eye
rising above the minor debris, but for
those under fire burning with grief, there's neither
fashion nor serenity. Bihzad captures
the moment before
my fears overwhelm me and I flee,
throwing my stupid hat to the ground.

Katabasis

Ten thousand left the high ground
and marched to the coast. . . . Unable
to contain our blood, the slippery
ground is flattened by our
departure. Our body
weight surprises us. Space
condenses but that's
not sea wind criss
crossing us, just bad
air exhumed from a charnel
house. Imagine a stranger's
oration, maybe a simple
stone in a valley tinted by a red sky,
an inscription
any scryer would appreciate, to set
what's crooked straight. Passing
through our bodies, we wormed
our way to day
break to boo
hoo over the open graves.

Acknowledgments

Many thanks to the editors of the journals and anthologies where these poems (some in earlier versions) first appeared:

Apalachee Review, "She Wants to Be Spanish"
Barrow Street Review, "Departure" and "Katabasis"
The Beloit Poetry Review, "Please Keep Hands Of* the
    Doors"
Bigger Than They Appear, "At the Terminal"
Blueline, "Black-Eyed Susans"
Bryant Literary Review, "The @'s of your %'s"
California Quarterly, "Reservations"
The Cape Rock, "Turning Red to Green Again" (as "A
    Saturday Mow")
Chirici, "Flor de Noche Buena"
Cloudbank, "Cryology" and "Indifference"
The Comstock Review, "The Murky Season" (as "All
    Night Murkiness")
Crab Creek Review, "The Invention of the Parachute"
    and "In Guo Xi's Early Spring"
Creeping Bent, "Ash"
Epoch, "My Mind Has Fallen from the Flowering Tree"
    (as "My Mind Fallen from a Flowering Tree")
Folio, "Trilobites"
Gargoyle, "Gloss" and "Caravaggio's Kimono"
Grey Sparrow, "Black Shines" (as "Shiners")
The Hamden-Sydney Poetry Review, "Another March" (as
    "In the Little Plazas")
Imagination and Place: Seasonings, "In Ankara I Smelled
    the Story of Lost Love"
Main Street Rag, "Finding the Bones of Birds in the
    Garden" (as "Finding Bones in the Garden"),

"Love in a Time of Drought," and "Making Love
      at Marconi Station"
Mediterranean Poetry, "Three Poems for Ahmet Ada"
      (as "Three for Ahmet Ada")
Milkwood Chronicle, "The Consolation of Biology"
The Missouri Review, "The Eurydice Chorus
New Letters, "According to the Baal Shem Toad"
The Pennsylvania Council of Teachers of English Bulletin,
      "Discontent in West Lafayette"
Philadelphia Stories, "Your Lucky Life," "Fooling the
      Angel," and "The Jewel of Berks County"
Poetry Now, "Locomotive"
Santa Clara Review, "Against Gardens"
Sequestrum, "Walnuts"
Silk Road, "Broken Triplets" (as "Triplet")
Verse, "A History of Water" (as "Watermarks")
Webster Review, "Somewhere Else You Are Getting
      Dressed" (as "Somewhere Else You're Getting
      Dressed")

Special thanks to Roger Weingarten, my extraordinary
editor, and to everyone at Longleaf Press.

Years of thanks to my son, Ben, whose patience and
technological abilities kept me in the 21st century and to
my wife, Elizabeth, who is everywhere present in these
pages.

About the Author

Ken Fifer is the author of four poetry collections: *After Fire*, March Street Press, 2007; *Water Presents*, Nova House Press, 2005; *The Moss That Rides on the Back of the Rock*, Mellen University Press, 1994; and *Falling Man*, Ithaca House, 1979. His poems have appeared in such journals as *Barrow Street, California Quarterly, Epoch, New Letters, The Literary Review, The Missouri Review, Ploughshares*. He has taught and read at conferences, poetry festivals, and universities from Ankara to Paris. A professor emeritus at Pennsylvania State University, he lives and works in Center Valley, Pennsylvania, with his wife and extended family, six dogs, two cats, and a parrot.

www.ingramcontent.com/pod-product-compliance
Lightning Source LLC
Chambersburg PA
CBHW020334130626
46549CB00003B/1170